"I'm not serving a menu, I'm serving a story. I'm serving my soul. I'm serving a conversation, and I want you to talk back to me."
- Dominique Crenn

Dominique Crenn is a celebrated French chef known

for her poetic and artistic approach to cooking. She made history as the first female chef in the U.S. to earn three Michelin stars for her San Francisco restaurant, Atelier Crenn. Crenn is also a passionate advocate for sustainability, equality, and storytelling through food, making her one of the most influential voices in the modern culinary world.

Table of Contents

A Note from the Author

This book was written with deep thought, countless reflections, and a heart full of passion. As my first ever book, at the very beginning of my journey as a chef it means everything to me. More than anything, I feel grateful.

Grateful for the trials that shaped me.
Grateful for the friends, mentors, and mistakes that taught me.
And grateful to *you*, for choosing to read something that comes from such an honest place.

If you're holding this book, I hope it does more than help you build menus. I hope it pushes you just a little to believe in your ideas. Because every one of us has something brilliant inside. Sometimes, all we need is that tiny nudge to put it out into the world.

So here's your push.

All the best, and I can't wait to see what *you* create. Looking forward to seeing you again in the next book.

– Maneesh Kumar

Introduction

Palate & Purpose didn't start with perfection.
It started in a small kitchen, with burnt rotis, uneven
salt, mismatched plates and a head full of dreams.

As a budding chef, I often found myself stuck between
inspiration and confusion. I wanted to serve food that
spoke, but I didn't know the language yet. I wanted to
build menus that made sense, that flowed, that hit the
heart not just filled the stomach.

This book isn't about fine dining or expensive wine
pairings. It's about learning how to **feel** your menu. It's
about curating meals with thought, matching dishes
with drinks that add meaning not just fizz. From simple
mocktails and regional coolers to bold infusions and
soulful starters, every chapter is a small step toward
turning food trials into personal triumphs.

You won't find perfection here.
But you'll find **purpose**.
And that's where every great plate begins.

Chapter 1: Menu Basics

A menu is far more than a list of dishes. It's the foundation of your identity as a chef. The first impression, the initial story, the promise you make with every plate. Every ingredient, every course, every flavor combination is a chapter in that story.

But how do you start?
How do you create a menu that speaks to both the diner and the chef?

In this chapter, we'll break down the basics of what makes a menu stand out. We'll cover everything from **seasonality** and **balance** to **cultural influence** and **cost management**. Let's turn the idea of a menu from a mere collection of items into an experience that diners will remember.

Understanding Seasonality

The heart of any great menu lies in knowing what's fresh and available. When you work with seasonal produce, you're not only getting the best flavor and nutrition, but you're also keeping your menu dynamic and affordable.

Why seasonality matters:

- **Flavor**: Fresh ingredients have the highest peak of flavor.

- **Cost**: Seasonal ingredients are more abundant and cheaper.

- **Creativity**: You'll be able to build your menu around what's exciting and fresh, not just what's "available."

Quick Tip:

A good practice is to build your menu around local, seasonal ingredients and then work outward to add elements that complement them. Consider local fish, farm to table vegetables, or seasonal fruits in desserts.

Balancing the Menu

Your menu needs to have **balance**. This means ensuring you're offering variety, texture, and color in each section, from appetizers to desserts.

- **Variety**: Combine different flavor profiles (sweet, savory, bitter, sour) and textures (crunchy, smooth, chewy).

- **Portion Sizes**: Balance light and heavy dishes. If you're offering a rich main course, you might want a lighter appetizer to start.

- **Vegetarian and Non Vegetarian Options**: Offer a range for diverse tastes, dietary preferences, and needs.

Sample Balance:

- **Appetizers**: A light, refreshing salad or an appetizer with contrasting textures (crispy and creamy).

- **Main Course**: Something hearty and satisfying like a braised dish or a rich curry, paired with grains like rice or bread.

- **Dessert**: A light sorbet or fruit-based dessert after a rich main course.

"I once thought more dishes meant a better menu, until I learned that too many choices overwhelm the eater."

Theme & Cultural Influence

Every great menu has a **theme**, even if it's subtle. A theme could be based on a region (e.g., Mediterranean), a season (e.g., summer lightness), or a particular cooking style (e.g., farm-to-table or street food-inspired).

Cultural Influence:

Don't be afraid to experiment with fusion, or to pull inspiration from your own heritage or travels. Pairing elements from different cuisines can create memorable flavor combinations that stand out. Just make sure the ingredients or techniques you choose make sense together.

Quick Tip:

Start small when mixing cuisines. For example, you might pair Italian pasta with Asian-inspired sauces or use South Indian spices in a Mediterranean dish. Taste is key!

Cost Management and Pricing

Pricing your menu isn't just about what your ingredients cost it's about offering value for both the diner and yourself. You need to ensure that each dish delivers the best taste while respecting your food costs.

- **Food Cost Percentage**: Aim for food cost percentages to fall within industry standards (around 30% for most dishes).

- **Portion Control**: Keeping portions consistent ensures you don't overserve or underserve, which could either cause waste or leave customers dissatisfied.

- **Menu Engineering**: Categorize dishes based on their profitability and popularity. Create a balanced mix of "stars" (high profit, high popularity) and "plow horses" (low profit, high popularity).

"Every menu tells a story. If yours doesn't, it's just a shopping list."

Chapter 2: Drink Pairing

A great meal doesn't end with the last bite of food it continues with the sip. Drinks are more than just refreshment; they're the perfect companion to your dishes, capable of enhancing flavors, providing contrast, and even shaping the entire dining experience.

Whether it's a light mocktail or a rich, spirit forward cocktail, drink pairing should be just as intentional as the menu itself. This chapter will guide you through the art of pairing drinks with your dishes, including **mocktails, cocktails, teas, coffees, and wines**. Together, we'll build a balanced selection of drinks that will not only complement your menu but also elevate your guests' entire experience.

Understanding the Basics of Pairing Drinks

Before we dive into specific drink options, let's cover the fundamentals of drink pairing. Think of it as a conversation between food and beverage, where the goal is balance and harmony.

- **Contrast vs. Complement**:
  When pairing, you can either **contrast** the flavors in a dish (e.g., pairing a rich, creamy dessert with a sharp, citrusy drink) or **complement** them (e.g., pairing a delicate white wine with a light seafood dish).

- **Intensity**:
  Make sure the intensity of the drink matches the dish. A strong, bold cocktail may overpower a delicate salad, while a light and refreshing

drink may fall flat against a rich, hearty main course.

- **Sweetness**:
  Sweet drinks, like fruit based mocktails or cocktails, work well with spicy or rich dishes, balancing heat and providing refreshment. For savory or sour dishes, try drinks that are more acidic or slightly bitter.

Quick Tip:
If in doubt, pair drinks based on the **dominant flavor** in the dish (spicy, sweet, sour, etc.). The right drink should highlight that flavor, not drown it out.

Mocktails: Refreshing & Creative Non-Alcoholic Pairings

Mocktails are more than just nonalcoholic alternatives they can be crafted with as much creativity and care as their alcoholic counterparts. Fresh herbs, fruits, and spices can turn a simple drink into a memorable experience.

Pairing Mocktails with Food:

- **Spicy Dishes**: Pair mocktails made with citrus (like lemon or lime) and a touch of honey or ginger to balance out the heat. Think of a **Citrus Ginger Fizz** with a spicy chili garlic stir-fry.

- **Fresh Salads or Light Dishes**: For lighter dishes, use refreshing herbs like mint, basil, or thyme in mocktails. A **Cucumber Mint Cooler** is perfect with a fresh summer salad.

- **Hearty, Rich Dishes**: For hearty dishes like tandoori meats, kebabs, or rich curries, create mocktails that bring in Indian flavors. A **Pomegranate and Tamarind Fizz** offers a tangy kick that pairs beautifully with grilled meats or roasted vegetables. Alternatively, a **Mint and Cucumber Cooler** with a touch of roasted cumin powder and black salt provides a refreshing contrast to spicy dishes like biryani or rich curries, while the cooling mint balances the heat.

Cocktails: Alcoholic Pairings with a Kick

Cocktails bring a different layer to pairing, combining flavors with the power of alcohol. They can either **cut through richness, enhance flavors,** or **balance spice**.

Pairing Cocktails with Food:

- **Light Dishes**: A classic **Gin and Tonic** or **Vodka Lemonade** works well with light salads, seafood, or sushi. The crispness of the gin complements the freshness of seafood, while vodka adds a bit of smoothness to a salad's acidity.

- **Rich Dishes**: Pair a **Whiskey Sour** or a **Negroni** with hearty meats or stews. The bold flavors in these cocktails stand up to the richness of the dish without overpowering it.

- **Spicy or Bold Flavors**: A **Margarita** or a **Mojito** pairs wonderfully with spicy Mexican or Asian dishes. The acidity of the lime in a Margarita helps tone down heat while complementing the flavors.

Teas and Coffees: The Unsung Heroes of Pairing

Teas and coffees might not always take center stage in food pairings, but they can bring unique complexity to a menu. They work especially well in **lighter courses** or **desserts** and can enhance the subtler flavors of the meal.

Pairing Teas and Coffees:

- **Green Tea**: Works beautifully with delicate, light dishes like sushi, salads, or seafood. The grassy notes of green tea cleanse the palate and prepare it for the next bite.

- **Black Tea**: Pairs wonderfully with spiced or roasted dishes, such as barbecue, grilled meats, or even curries. Try pairing a smoky **Assam Tea** with a spiced lamb dish.

- **Coffee**: Great with rich desserts like chocolate cake or tiramisu. The bitterness of coffee balances out the sweetness of the dessert. Try pairing a **Cappuccino** with a creamy tiramisu or a **Espresso** with a dark chocolate mousse.

Wine Pairings: The Classic Companion

While wine might seem like a "fancier" option, it doesn't have to be reserved for the elite. Wine is an accessible pairing tool when done correctly. Whether it's a **light white** or a **bold red**, wine has a way of accentuating the flavors in a dish.

Basic Wine Pairing Guide:

- **White Wines**: Light, crisp white wines (like Sauvignon Blanc or Chardonnay) pair well with seafood, chicken, and salads. They enhance the freshness and lightness of the dishes.

- **Red Wines**: Heavier reds (like Cabernet Sauvignon or Merlot) pair beautifully with rich meats, steaks, and tomato-based dishes. The tannins in red wine help cut through the fat in meat.

- **Rosé and Sparkling Wines**: Great for salads, light pasta, and appetizers. The bubbles in sparkling wines like Prosecco also work well to cleanse the palate between bites.

Thoughtful Pairings at Kappa Chakka Kandhari

Chef **Regi Mathew**, the visionary behind *Kappa Chakka Kandhari*, is known for his relentless dedication to preserving and elevating Kerala's traditional cuisine. A seasoned chef with over three decades in the culinary industry, Regi left behind a global corporate kitchen career to chase his roots. With KCK, he set out to document and serve more than 800 heirloom recipes from across Kerala, sourced straight from home cooks and regional kitchens.

One of his most compelling culinary philosophies lies in how food and beverages harmonize. At KCK, the drink menu doesn't just quench thirst it tells a parallel story of Kerala's bold, bright, and balanced flavors.

- **The Absolute Kandhari**, for instance, is a fiery refresher infused with bird's eye chilli (locally known as kandhari mulaku). This drink isn't just heat it's **layered with citrusy sharpness and subtle sweetness**, making it the perfect pairing for rich, coconut-heavy dishes like **Mutton Coconut Fry** or **Prawn Kizhi**.

- For those who enjoy a mellow touch, **Nannari Sharbat** a traditional drink made from the root of Indian sarsaparilla is served chilled and sweet. Its cooling nature perfectly **balances spicy mains**, providing a natural reset between bites of something like **Beef Ularthiyathu**.

- And then there's **Goli Soda**, the nostalgic glass-bottled fizz with a marble stopper. Light, fizzy, and tangy, it cuts through the sour and umami flavors of dishes like **Neimeen Nellika Masala Fry**, heightening the experience while taking diners down memory lane.

Chef Regi's approach shows how **pairing drinks isn't about alcohol or mocktails alone it's about bringing thought and heart into every element on the table**.

Chapter 3: The Art of Presentation

As a chef, you know that the taste of your food is paramount. But what's the first thing that diners experience when they sit down to eat? The visual appeal of your dish. The art of presentation can elevate your cooking from good to unforgettable. In this chapter, we'll dive into how you can make your dishes as beautiful as they are delicious.

Why Presentation Matters

The way food is presented can have a profound impact on the overall dining experience. A beautifully plated dish stimulates the senses, creates anticipation, and often enhances the perceived taste of the meal. It's also an opportunity for you as a chef to express creativity, showcase technique, and tell a story through your food.

Key Points:

- **First Impressions Matter**: We eat with our eyes first. A well-presented dish can excite the senses and set the tone for the meal.

- **Engagement**: Good presentation encourages diners to engage with the dish in a thoughtful way. It invites them to savor the moment.

- **Reflection of Quality**: A thoughtfully plated dish reflects the care and attention you put into your cooking.

Plating Techniques

Plating can seem intimidating, but with a few fundamental techniques, you can master it. The goal is not to overwhelm the dish with too much decoration, but to complement the food in a way that highlights its beauty.

Here are some essential plating techniques:

- **The Rule of Thirds**: Divide your plate into sections and arrange your food in a balanced way, not simply in the center. This creates a dynamic visual flow.

- **Height and Layering**: Adding height to your plate makes it feel more dynamic. You can create this effect by stacking ingredients (like a tower of roasted vegetables or a layered salad) or by using tools like ring molds to shape components.

- **Negative Space**: Don't be afraid of leaving some empty space on the plate. Negative space makes the dish feel clean and allows the food to stand out.

- **Garnishing**: Garnishes should enhance the dish in both flavor and visual appeal. Fresh herbs, edible flowers, or even a swirl of sauce can add color and texture. But remember, less is more don't over garnish.

Quick Tip:
The sauce should never just be dumped on the plate. Instead, use a spoon to create beautiful drizzles, dots, or swirls. A little creativity goes a long way!

The Power of Color

Colors play an important role in presentation. A well plated dish uses a palette of contrasting colors to create visual interest. Think about the colors of vegetables, proteins, sauces, and garnishes working together to create a feast for the eyes.

- **Contrast**: A green garnish on a red dish, or a vibrant yellow sauce on a white plate, creates a beautiful contrast.

- **Complementary Colors**: Pair colors from the opposite sides of the color wheel for maximum impact. Red and green, for example, are complementary colors that pop next to each other.

- **Balance**: Aim to balance the bright, bold colors with more neutral tones, like the brown of roasted meat or the creaminess of a sauce.

Quick Tip:
Use a white plate as your canvas. It makes the food's colors pop and allows the focus to be on your dish, rather than the background.

The Importance of Texture

Texture isn't just about the food it's also about the presentation. Layering textures in your plating adds depth and makes the dish more interesting. Consider pairing a crispy element with something creamy, or contrasting a smooth purée with something crunchy.

- **Crisp and Crunchy**: Think fried shallots on a creamy curry or a crisp wonton skin on a soft filling.

- **Smooth and Velvety**: Use a smooth sauce, creamy risotto, or a velvety mousse to create richness.

- **Chewy and Tender**: Grilled vegetables, slow cooked meats, or soft noodles add a chewy element that contrasts with other textures.

Regional Influences in Presentation

As an Indian chef, you may want to explore how the visual aesthetics of traditional Indian cuisine can be incorporated into modern plating. Indian cuisine is often served on flat, round platters like **thalis** or even traditional **banana leaves**. These serve not just as functional, but also as cultural and visual tools.

- **Thali style Presentation**: Serve your dishes on a **thali**, with small portions of different curries, grains, and sides, showcasing diversity on one plate.

- **Banana Leaf**: For a more rustic, traditional approach, serve the food on a banana leaf, which not only adds color but also an earthy, aromatic touch.

Quick Tip:
For a more modern twist, consider plating a **fusion dish** on a thali style platter with a contemporary flair. This

creates an interesting juxtaposition of traditional and modern aesthetics.

Chef Massimo Bottura is one of the most influential
and innovative chefs of our time, known for his **creative**

reinterpretation of traditional Italian cuisine. As the chef-owner of **Osteria Francescana** in Modena, Italy, he has earned three Michelin stars and worldwide acclaim for his artful dishes that challenge conventional culinary norms. Bottura's approach is not just about flavors but about storytelling through food. His work often combines **historical references, contemporary twists, and humor**, reflecting a deep understanding of culture and history while pushing the boundaries of gastronomy.

One of his most iconic dishes, **"Oops! I Dropped the Lemon Tart,"** is a brilliant example of how **presentation can tell a story** and challenge expectations. The dish is presented as if a **lemon tart has been "dropped,"** with the tart scattered messily on the plate. The seemingly imperfect dish represents **creativity, spontaneity, and the beauty in flaws**. Bottura explains that the dish was inspired by the idea of imperfection in the world things don't always go as planned, and that's where true **creativity and innovation can be found**. This dish pushes the idea that **imperfection can be a form of art**, and it encourages diners to embrace the unexpected beauty of mistakes.

The dish has been celebrated for its boldness and **how it flips the notion of perfection** in fine dining, teaching that presentation doesn't need to be rigid or symmetrical it can be messy, playful, and expressive.

Chapter 4: Creating Signature Dishes

As a budding chef, one of the most exciting aspects of your career is creating dishes that not only reflect your style but also leave a lasting impression on your guests. Signature dishes are more than just recipes they are a reflection of your creativity, passion, and skill. In this chapter, we'll explore how you can develop your own signature dishes that stand out and resonate with your guests.

What Makes a Signature Dish?

A signature dish is a creation that defines you as a chef. It's a dish that people associate with your style and expertise. But what makes a dish stand out?

- **Uniqueness**: It should be something that isn't easily replicated. It could be a twist on a classic dish, or something completely innovative.

- **Consistency**: A signature dish must be executed flawlessly every time. Consistency in taste, presentation, and quality is key.

- **Memorability**: When guests try it, they should be able to remember it long after they've finished the meal.

Think of it as your culinary "calling card." It should capture your essence as a chef.

Finding Inspiration

Your signature dish should feel personal, but where do you draw inspiration from? Here are some ways to get started:

- **Cultural Influence**: Your roots and heritage can play a huge role in the creation of your dish. Infuse elements of your culture or family recipes with your own modern twists.

- **Personal Experiences**: Whether it's a dish from your childhood, a memorable meal you had while traveling, or a new ingredient you've recently discovered, inspiration often comes from the stories we carry with us.

- **Food Trends**: Keep an eye on global food trends, but make sure you're adding your own unique spin to them. Whether it's plantbased cuisine or global fusion, these trends can give you a direction to start in.

- **Seasonal Ingredients**: Seasonal produce can influence your signature dishes. A dish that highlights fresh, inseason ingredients not only showcases your culinary knowledge but also allows you to take advantage of the best flavors nature has to offer.**The Process of Creating Your Signature Dish**

Now that you have your inspiration, it's time to get creative. Here's a stepbystep process to help you develop your dish:

1. **Start with a Concept**
   Think about what you want your dish to

represent. Is it a story you want to tell? Or perhaps a memory you want to evoke? Start by deciding the concept behind the dish.

2. **Choose Your Ingredients**
   Select ingredients that align with your concept. Choose them for flavor, texture, and how well they'll work together. Don't be afraid to experiment with new ingredients or combinations.

3. **Focus on Technique**
   The way you prepare and cook your ingredients is just as important as the flavors. Whether you're slowcooking meat, creating a smooth puree, or perfecting the art of tempering spices, the techniques you use will set your dish apart.

4. **Balance of Flavors and Textures**
   A great dish balances a range of flavors and texturessweet, salty, bitter, sour, and umami. Incorporate various textures, from crispy to creamy, to add depth to the dish.

5. **Presentation**
   How you present the dish is just as important as what's on the plate. Think about color contrasts, garnishes, and the overall layout. Remember, less is often more, so keep it simple but striking.

6. **Test and Refine**
   Once you've created the dish, test it multiple times. Get feedback from colleagues, mentors,

and friends. Refine the recipe, the presentation, and the flavor until it's perfect.

Examples of Signature Dishes

Here are a few examples of signature dishes that have made a mark in the culinary world, showcasing innovation, creativity, and bold flavors:

- **Mango and Saffron Chicken**: Created by Chef **Manish Mehrotra**, this fusion dish features juicy chicken marinated in a mango and saffron yogurt sauce, grilled to perfection, and served with a tangy tamarind chutney. The richness of saffron and the sweetness of mango come together to create a memorable and vibrant flavor profile that perfectly represents Chef Mehrotra's modern take on Indian cuisine.

- **Spiced Kheer with Pistachio Crumble**: This inventive dessert comes from **Chef Gaggan Anand**, who has redefined traditional Indian sweets. His modern twist on kheer combines creamy rice pudding flavored with cardamom, saffron, and cinnamon, topped with a pistachio crumble and a sprinkle of rose petals. It's a perfect example of how Chef Anand blends traditional flavors with contemporary techniques to elevate classic Indian desserts.

- **Tandoori Cauliflower Steak: Chef Suvir Saran**, known for his vegetarian creations, brings a smoky and spicy twist to cauliflower. His Tandoori Cauliflower Steak is marinated in a rich tandoori masala, grilled to golden perfection, and served with a refreshing cucumber raita and a dash of pomegranate seeds for added color and crunch. This dish is a bold, Indianinspired vegetarian option with layers of flavor and texture.

- **Ant Bite (Ant Pavlova)**: A truly innovative creation from **Chef Johnson Ebenezer** at Farmlore, the Ant Pavlova, or "Ant Bite," is a dessert that takes foraged ingredients to the next level. The pavlova is topped with ants, providing a tangy and crunchy contrast to the sweet meringue. This dish challenges conventional thinking and plays with the boundaries of culinary creativity, blending sustainability and daring flavors to create something entirely unique.

These dishes are perfect examples of how chefs around the world are pushing boundaries while staying rooted in tradition. They show that a signature dish isn't just about flavorit's about telling a story, experimenting with new ingredients, and creating an experience for your guests.

Refining and Perfecting Your Dish

Your signature dish is a work in progress, and there's always room for improvement. Constantly taste, tweak, and refine your dishes. It's important to keep experimenting and challenging yourself to perfect the flavor and presentation.

- **Refining Taste**: Ensure your dish has the right balance of flavors. Taste as you cook, and don't be afraid to adjust seasoning, add acidity, or tweak spices.

- **Feedback**: Don't hesitate to ask others for their feedback whether it's your colleagues, mentors, or customers. The more input you get, the more you'll be able to finetune your dish.

- **Consistency**: Make sure your signature dish is repeatable. Practice your technique until it becomes second nature.

When Simplicity Wasn't Enough And What I Did About It

The First Attempt
Back in my **first semester of college**, my friend **Milton** and I entered a *Cooking Without Fire* competition at **Indian Academy College**. We came up with an elegant idea a **creamy cucumber salad**, delicately swirled, stacked, and topped with a smooth dressing. The judges tasted it and shared kind feedback. But... we didn't win.

At first, it stung. But then I looked around—there were **20 to 30 teams**, many with **three to four different dishes**, displaying variety, skill, and more complexity. Our single cucumber dish, no matter how well executed, didn't carry the weight.

The Comeback

The following year, we returned to the same competition—but this time with a **strategy and story**. Our menu included:

- **Shea Muesli Bircher**, beautifully presented in a **coconut shell**

- **Som Tam** (raw papaya salad)

- **Spiced Watermelon Salad**

This time, we offered **variety in texture, ingredients, and techniques**. We were no longer "the cucumber guys"—we were chefs with a plan, presentation, and purpose. And yes, **we won**.

That experience taught me something I carry into every menu now:

A dish should not just be tasty—it should be intentional, layered, and thoughtful. A well-told story on a plate stands out.

Chapter 5: Curating Menus for Different Occasions

A well curated menu isn't just a list of dishes it's a journey.
It sets the mood, matches the vibe of the event, and speaks to the heart of the people you're serving. Whether you're designing a menu for an intimate gathering, a big fat wedding, a corporate lunch, or a popup event, the right combination of dishes and drinks can leave a lasting impression.

In this chapter, we'll explore how to thoughtfully craft menus for various occasions, balancing flavors, styles, and guest expectations.

Understanding the Occasion

Before you even think about the food, step back and ask:

- What's the occasion?

- What is the mood or theme?

- Who are the guests?

Each event demands a different kind of energy.
For example:

- **Weddings** need grand, indulgent menus filled with a mix of traditional and contemporary dishes.

- **Casual brunches** are about light, fresh, and colorful foods.

- **Corporate events** call for a smart balance nothing too messy or heavy, but still impressive and satisfying.

Your menu should *feel* like it belongs to the event. Think of it as dressing appropriately but with your own flair.

Structuring a Menu for the Event

When crafting a menu, think of it like a story with a clear beginning, a satisfying middle, and a memorable end. Each course should complement the next, creating flow and rhythm. A common rookie mistake is to overload the menu or repeat similar flavor profiles. Let's break it down:

Starters / Appetizers

This is the first impression keep it light, exciting, and textured. Go for variety:

- One fried (like *Mini Samosas* or *Cheese Corn Balls*)

- One grilled or baked (like *Tandoori Prawns* or *Stuffed Mushrooms*)

- One refreshing (like *Papdi Chaat Bites* or *Melon & Feta Skewers*)

Main Course

Balance is key include at least one dish from each of the following:

- **Protein based** (Chicken, Fish, Paneer, or Tofu)

- **Grain or carb** (Rice, Biryani, Couscous, Millet, or Pasta)

- **Vegetable hero** (Seasonal curry, grilled veggie medley)

- **Bread** (Roti, Paratha, or Garlic Naan)

- **Gravy vs Dry**: Don't serve only dry or only gravy dishes mix both so the plate doesn't feel flat.

Desserts

Keep this thoughtful, not just sweet. Match sweetness with texture or acidity:

- Traditional like *Rasmalai, Moong Dal Halwa*

- Fusion like *Gulab Jamun Cheesecake* or *Masala Chai Panna Cotta*

- A light fruit based option for balance (*Fruit Tartlets* or *Rose Milk Granita*)

Drinks

Base your drink pairing on the vibe of the food and season.
Mocktails, coolers, spiced infusions, or lassis can work wonders. For example:

- *Aam Panna* with summer thalis

- *Kokum Cooler* with spicy Konkani dishes

- *Sparkling Nimbu Shikanji* for brunch menus

Sample Menus for Different Occasions

Below are curated sample menus for various types of events to help you get started. Each is crafted with balance, flavor harmony, and guest experience in mind.

1. Sunday Brunch with Friends

Vibe: Light, fun, colorful – a mix of global & Indian flavors

Starters:

- Mini Masala Croissants

- Avocado Sev Puri

- Watermelon & Feta Bites with Balsamic Drizzle

Main Course:

- Mushroom & Cheese Frittata

- Millet Upma with Coconut Chutney

- Grilled Herb Chicken with Lemon Butter Sauce

- Garlic Naan Sliders (Paneer or Chicken Tikka)

Desserts:

- Filter Coffee Panna Cotta

- Fresh Mango Slices with Chilli Salt

Drinks:

- Sparkling Jaljeera Cooler

- Cold Brew with Cardamom

2. Traditional Indian Wedding Buffet

Vibe: Rich, festive, nostalgic with grandeur

Starters:

- Tandoori Aloo & Malai Broccoli
- Chicken Reshmi Kebab
- Dahi Bhalla Shots with Pomegranate

Main Course:

- Dum Biryani (Veg/Chicken)
- Dal Makhani & Shahi Paneer
- Laal Maas (Rajasthani mutton curry)
- Jeera Rice & Garlic Naan

Desserts:

- Gulab Jamun Cheesecake
- Rabdi Jalebi
- Ice Cream Bar with Indian Toppings

Drinks:

- Rose Sherbet with Basil Seeds
- Buttermilk Shots with Curry Leaf Foam

Food Trial Menu for Budding Chefs

Vibe: Experimental, cost effective, concept driven

Starters:

- Banana Stem Croquettes with Beetroot Chutney

- Smoked Mutton Sukka Tartlets

- Corn & Curry Leaf Soup Shots

Main Course:

- Chilli Jackfruit Bao

- Steamed Rice with Gongura Paneer

- Pesto Khichdi with Parmesan Crisp

- Citrus & Spice Chicken Roulade

Desserts:

- Deconstructed Motichoor Ladoo Mousse

- Chocolate Chikki with Sea Salt

Drinks:

- Spiced Nimbu Kombucha

- Mango Ginger Fizz

Each of these menus is just a base tweak it to match the crowd, budget, and seasonal ingredients. The goal is always the same: leave your guests feeling seen, satisfied, and surprised.

Chef Johnson Ebenezer

In a quiet corner of Bengaluru, far away from the chaos of city life, Chef Johnson Ebenezer isn't just cooking—he's curating time. At **Farmlore**, his experiential restaurant built on a seven-acre farm, the menu is never printed, never fixed, and never the same. Instead, it is a reflection of the soil beneath his feet, the rain in the air, and the stories he wants to tell.

When curating menus for different occasions, Chef Johnson doesn't begin with a protein or a starch. He begins with a memory. A feeling. A conversation with the land.

One season, he served a dish called **Seataphor**, inspired by the plight of the oceans—Kochi snapper laid on a sea of contrasting sauces: one clean, one polluted. It was art. It was protest. It was plated poetry.

For festive occasions, his menus are filled with bold, indulgent flavors—like **Bannur Bun Broth**, a tribute to Karnataka's Bannur lamb, slowly smoked over two days and paired with fluffy buns soaked in rich stock, served when the clouds roll in and the monsoon mood hits the soul.

For lighthearted garden lunches, he leans towards fermented jackfruit, local grains, floral broths—playful, surprising, intimate.

Each menu is an act of curation—not just of ingredients, but of emotion. Like setting a table for a memory yet to be made.

Chef Johnson reminds us:
Menus are not written. They are grown.

Chapter 6: The Basics of Food Costing

GOLDEN FORMULA

Food Cost % = (Cost of Ingredients / Selling Price) × 100

Your ideal food cost percentage varies depending on the setup, but a common industry benchmark is **28–35%** for profitability.

Example 1: Masala Pani Puri (Street Food Twist)

- **Ingredient Cost:** ₹12 (puri, spiced water, filling, garnishes)

- **Ideal Food Cost %:** 25%

- **Selling Price = ₹12 ÷ 0.25 = ₹48**
  In a modern café, you could price it at ₹55–₹65 with a gourmet twist and plating.

Example 2: Butter Chicken with Garlic Naan

- **Ingredient Cost:** ₹120 (boneless chicken, makhani gravy ingredients, butter, naan, garnish)

- **Ideal Food Cost %:** 30%

- **Selling Price = ₹120 ÷ 0.30 = ₹400**
  You can charge more if served in a fine dining setup with a side salad or raita.

Example 3: Quinoa & Roasted Veg Salad with Lemon Dressing

- **Ingredient Cost:** ₹60 (quinoa, zucchini, bell peppers, lettuce, lemon, olive oil)

- **Ideal Food Cost %:** 28%

- **Selling Price = ₹60 ÷ 0.28 ≈ ₹215**
  Premium because of health focused crowd and imported ingredients.

Example 4: Filter Coffee Tiramisu (Fusion Dessert)

- **Ingredient Cost:** ₹70 (mascarpone, cream, coffee decoction, sponge, cocoa)

- **Ideal Food Cost %:** 30%

- **Selling Price = ₹70 ÷ 0.30 = ₹233**
  Desserts offer great profit margins if plated smartly.

Example 5: Aam Panna Mojito (Mocktail)

- **Ingredient Cost:** ₹25 (raw mango, mint, soda, sugar, spice mix)

- **Ideal Food Cost %:** 25%

- **Selling Price = ₹25 ÷ 0.25 = ₹100**
  Mocktails have huge potential for upselling. Add flair to garnish or serve in signature glassware.

How to Decide Your Ideal Food Cost %

1. Know Your Setup Type

Type of Business	Ideal Food Cost %
Street Food Stall	20–25%
Casual Café/Cloud Kitchen	25–30%
Mid-Range Restaurant	28–32%
Fine Dining	30–35%
Premium/Plated Tasting	35–40% (sometimes)

As you go higher in experience, service, and ambience your margins adjust accordingly.

2. Check Your Overheads & Target Profit

If your rent, salaries, and utility bills are high, you'll need more margin so lower food cost %. If you're operating from a low-cost setup (home kitchen, popup, or college trial), you can afford a slightly higher food cost and still make a good profit.

3. Look at Competition

- Are they pricing a similar dish at ₹250? Then your ₹600 fine dine plate may not sell unless it's exceptional.

- You don't always have to be cheaper but you must give *value for money.*

4. Decide Based on Dish Type

Dish Type	Typical Cost %
Drinks / Mocktails	10–20%
Starters	25–30%
Mains	28–35%
Desserts	20–25%
Fusion/Experimental	30–40%

5. Use This Formula to Reverse Calculate

Selling Price = Ingredient Cost ÷ Ideal Food Cost %

Example:
If ingredient cost is ₹80 and your target is 30% food cost

₹80 ÷ 0.30 = ₹266.67 → round to ₹270

Common Mistake: "I thought I had to multiply..."

Let's be honest **a lot of us mess this up at first.** You think, "Okay, my food cost percentage is 30%, so I'll multiply my ingredient cost with 0.30 and get the selling price."
But hold up that's **not** how it works.

Here's how I learned it myself:

If your **ingredient cost is ₹60**, and your **ideal food cost % is 30%**,
you might think:

₹60 × 0.30 = ₹18

But wait... ₹18 is just a small part of ₹60. That's not your **price**, right?

Now here's the truth: You're supposed to **divide** your ingredient cost by your ideal food cost %, because that % is what part of the **final price** you're spending on ingredients.

 The real formula:

Selling Price = Ingredient Cost ÷ Food Cost %

So now:

₹60 ÷ 0.30 = ₹200

Boom! That ₹60 becomes 30% of ₹200.
That's your ideal selling price.

Remember this shortcut:

- If you want to **find the price, divide.**

- If you want to **set a budget for ingredients, multiply.**

Key Elements in Food Costing:

- **Ingredient Cost (including waste & trimming)**

- **Packaging Cost (for delivery/takeaway)**

- **Garnishes & Hidden Costs (butter for basting, cooking oil, etc.)**

- **Overheads (gas, electricity, water shared cost)**

- **Labour (in advanced setups)**

Always account for everything even the spoon of ghee or a sprig of mint!

How to Price a Dish Smartly

Pricing isn't just about multiplying cost it's also about:

- **Perceived value:** Would someone pay ₹200 for your dish if it *looks* and *tastes* like ₹300?

- **Competition pricing:** Know what similar places are charging.

- **Audience psychology:** ₹199 often sells better than ₹200. Round pricing works better in fine dining, quirky ones in cafés.

-

Menu Engineering Basics

Use the **4 Quadrant Rule** for each dish:

Type	Description
Stars	High profit, high popularity (Keep them shining!)
Plow horses	Low profit, high popularity (Find ways to cut cost or upsell sides)
Puzzles	High profit, low popularity (Change presentation or placement on menu)
Dogs	Low profit, low popularity (Consider replacing)

Hidden Money Mistakes Young Chefs Make

- Not weighing ingredients while costing

- Ignoring seasonal fluctuations in prices

- Overdecorating or overserving portions

- Forgetting packaging & delivery platform cuts

- Not testing the dish for consistency over 3–4 trials

Chapter 7: Setting Up Your Tasting & Trial Kitchen

Because great dishes are born from messy counters and clean intentions.

Why You Need a Trial Kitchen

Every chef needs a space to play. This isn't about fancy equipment or five-star setups. This is where:

- Recipes fail and then succeed.

- You taste, adjust, and repeat.

- You find what works and what doesn't.

This space helps you:

- Develop your **signature dishes**.

- Experiment with **pairings**.

- Understand **timing, textures, and presentation**.

Basic Equipment Checklist (Home or College Setup)

Essentials	Why You Need It
Gas Stove / Induction	Core heat source
Mixing Bowls (varied sizes)	For marination, mixing batters, etc.
Nonstick & Cast Iron Pans	Versatility and heat control

Essentials	Why You Need It
Weighing Scale & Measuring Cups	Accuracy for trials
Blender / Mixer Grinder	For purées, sauces, chutneys
Baking Tray & Oven (OTG)	Optional, for baked experiments
Plating Tweezers / Spoons	Precision in plating
Cutting Board + Good Knives	Safe and efficient prep
Ice Tray / Shaker	For mocktail trials

Start with what you have. Upgrade as you grow.

Setting Up Your Station

Organize your space into zones:

1. **Prep Zone**: Chopping board, knives, marination bowls.

2. **Cooking Zone**: Stove, spatulas, pans.

3. **Tasting & Plating Zone**: Empty space, garnishes, plating tools.

4. **Mocktail/Drink Corner**: If you're testing drinks, set up a small bar area with glasses, shakers, syrups, etc.

Your Trial Journal (Nonnegotiable!)

Document everything:

- What you cooked.

- Quantities used.

- What worked.

- What didn't.

- Honest tasting notes.

- Feedback from friends/family.

Your future signature dishes will be born from the scribbles in this book.

Pro Tip: Test in Small Batches

You don't need to make 10 portions every time. Cook in small quantities2 to 4 servings max. It saves ingredients, time, and your energy.

Chapter 8: Designing Your First Menu

Crafting a menu isn't just about picking dishes it's about creating an experience.

The Essence of Menu Design

Designing a menu isn't just about listing dishes; it's about creating an experience for your diners from the moment they lay eyes on it. Every dish, every ingredient, and every flavor must tell a story. You're not just cooking; you're designing a journey for the palate.

Here's a simple framework for building your first menu:

1. Know Your Theme and Audience

Before you even think about ingredients, understand the kind of food you want to serve.

- **Is your menu seasonal?**
- **Do you want to focus on comfort food, gourmet, or fusion?**
- **Is there a cultural or personal story behind your menu?**

If your theme is **traditional Indian cuisine**, that will influence your flavor profile, choice of spices, and overall style. If it's **modern fusion**, you'll experiment more with innovative ingredients and plating.

let's imagine a scenario where you're setting up a **fusion restaurant** that combines **traditional Indian flavors with contemporary cooking techniques**. You want to create a menu that honors the rich culinary heritage of India but with a modern, fresh twist perfect for an audience that appreciates innovation but also loves the comfort of traditional food.

Scenario: Fusion Indian Cuisine "Roots & Revelations"

Theme:

The theme of the restaurant is to bring the **depth of Indian flavors** into a modern, contemporary setting. The food will incorporate **traditional Indian spices** and ingredients but will be served in an unconventional, elegant way. Think **traditional thalis** reinvented as tapas or **classic curries** served in unique bowls or jars. The menu will appeal to people who enjoy the familiar but are open to the new and exciting.

Audience:

- Young professionals, foodies, and travelers who love to experiment with their palate but appreciate traditional comfort.

- Diners who are adventurous but have a strong emotional connection to the flavors of India.

- People who are health conscious, with an interest in using organic or sustainably sourced ingredients.

Sample Menu for "Roots & Revelations"

Appetizers:

1. **Masala Chaat Tacos**
   Crisp taco shells filled with a spiced potato mixture, chickpeas, and topped with tamarind chutney and yogurt foam. A fusion of Mexican and Indian street food.

2. **Tandoori Chicken Sliders**
   Minced tandoori chicken, lightly spiced, grilled to perfection, served on a soft bun with a tangy mint chutney and pickled onions.

3. **Saffron & Cashew Hummus with Pita Chips**
   A traditional Middle Eastern dip infused with saffron and roasted cashews, served with freshly baked pita chips.

Mains:

1. **Peshawari Naan Pizza**
   A thin naan base topped with creamy yogurt, slow cooked lamb, and aromatic Peshawari spices. Finished with a sprinkle of fresh coriander and cashew nuts.

2. **Mango and Turmeric Glazed Grilled Salmon**
   Fresh salmon grilled to perfection, marinated in a mango turmeric glaze, served with cumin spiced quinoa and a side of tangy green chutney.

3. **Rogan Josh Bao**
   Soft bao buns filled with tender lamb cooked in
   a rich rogan josh curry sauce, garnished with
   fresh mint and a touch of saffron.

Desserts:

1. **Gulab Jamun Cheesecake**
   A modern twist on the classic Indian sweet rich,
   creamy cheesecake infused with gulab jamun
   syrup, topped with pistachio crumbs.

2. **Spiced Chia Pudding with Rosewater Syrup**
   A creamy chia pudding infused with cardamom
   and cinnamon, topped with rosewater syrup
   and pistachio dust for a floral finish.

Drinks:

1. **Coconut & Curry Leaf Mojito**
   A tropical mojito with a twist, made with fresh
   coconut water, rum, and a hint of curry leaf,
   garnished with fresh lime.

2. **Mango Lassi Martini**
   A fusion of the classic mango lassi and a martini,
   with a mix of mango puree, yogurt, and vodka,
   topped with a touch of saffron.

This menu is inspired by the **vision of Chef Manish Mehrotra**, a renowned name in Indian fusion cuisine. Chef Mehrotra, the executive chef at **Indian Accent** in New Delhi, is famous for his innovative approach to Indian food, blending traditional flavors with contemporary techniques and presentations. His dishes often incorporate global culinary trends while celebrating India's rich culinary heritage.

In this menu, I've drawn upon his style of **fusion cooking**, where he uses traditional Indian ingredients and reimagines them in fresh, modern ways. For example, his approach to **reinterpreting street food** and **elevating traditional dishes** is reflected in items like the **Masala Chaat Tacos** and the **Rogan Josh Bao**, offering a unique dining experience that is familiar yet new.

Explanation:

- The **Masala Chaat Tacos** blend the crispness of a Mexican taco with the familiar tangy, spicy flavors of Indian chaat, making it a perfect example of how comfort food can be twisted into something new.

- The **Peshawari Naan Pizza** takes the traditional naan and transforms it into a pizza style base offering a unique twist on the classic flavors of Peshawar with a fusion of Italian and Indian elements.

- The **Rogan Josh Bao** brings the iconic Kashmiri curry into a soft Chinese bao bun, creating a bite sized, handheld version of the famous dish.

Why this works:

The menu is designed to be **bold** but **familiar** people who love Indian food will find comforting elements, while those looking for something new and innovative will be drawn to the modern presentation and unexpected pairings.

It captures the **fusion theme** by blending traditional flavors with techniques and presentation styles from different cuisines, creating a menu that is both **comforting and exciting**, appealing to those who enjoy food that's both nostalgic and forward thinking.

2. Balance the Menu

A good menu has balance not only in flavor but in variety. You want to create a balanced dining experience, with enough options but not overwhelming your guests. Consider these aspects:

- **Appetizers:** Light, exciting, and meant to awaken the palate.

- **Mains:** The heart of the meal rich, satisfying, and filling.

- **Desserts:** Light, refreshing, or indulgent, depending on the meal.

- **Drinks:** Offer both alcoholic and nonalcoholic options. Try a mix of mocktails, soft drinks, and something unique (e.g., fresh fruit sodas).

- **Specials:** Seasonal offerings or chef's special dishes that make the menu feel fresh and evolving.

Let's break down each section:

1. Appetizers:

Purpose: Appetizers are designed to **awaken the palate** and set the tone for the meal. They should be light, flavorful, and tease the senses without filling up your guests too early.

Considerations:

- **Flavors:** Use appetizers to introduce bold or complex flavors, but keep the textures light.

- **Portion Sizes:** Small portions that can be shared, allowing guests to sample a variety.

- **Variety:** Offer a mix of **hot and cold, crunchy and smooth** textures, and **spicy or tangy** flavors.

Example:

- **Mango & Chilli Prawns:** A tangy twist on traditional prawns, infused with a touch of chili and sweet mango salsa, served on a small skewer for easy sharing.

- **Papdi Chaat with Tamarind Foam:** A modern take on the classic Indian street snack, served as a deconstructed plate with crispy papdi and a refreshing tamarind foam.

2. Mains:

Purpose: The main course is the heart of the meal **rich, satisfying**, and filling. This is where your guests will experience the **full-bodied flavors** of your menu.

Considerations:

- **Protein and Vegetables:** Ensure that the mains offer a good balance of meat, seafood, and vegetarian options.

- **Satisfying but not overwhelming:** The portion sizes should be hearty but not so large that they cause discomfort.

- **Flavor Balance:** Mains should incorporate both **rich, indulgent flavors** (e.g., creamy curries, slow cooked meats) and **lighter options** (e.g., grilled fish or vegetable-based dishes).

Example:

- **Butter Chicken with Cashew Gravy:** A rich, indulgent dish featuring succulent chicken in a creamy, cashew-based gravy, served with garlic naan.

- **Kale & Quinoa Kofta:** A healthy yet filling vegetarian option, offering a blend of superfoods like kale and quinoa, combined with a fragrant spice mix and served with a tangy yogurt sauce.

3. Desserts:

Purpose: Desserts can either be light and refreshing to cleanse the palate or indulgent and rich to end the meal on a high note.

Considerations:

- **Type of Dessert:** Balance indulgent, rich desserts with lighter, refreshing options to cater to different preferences.

- **Seasonal Flavors:** Use fruits and ingredients that are in season to keep things fresh.

- **Textures:** Mix up the textures from creamy to crunchy, warm to cold, and rich to light.

Example:

- **Gulab Jamun Cheesecake:** A fusion of two beloved desserts rich, creamy cheesecake topped with delicate gulab jamun syrup.

- **Pistachio & Rosewater Kulfi:** A light and refreshing frozen dessert, flavored with pistachio and rosewater for a fragrant finish to the meal.

4. Drinks:

Purpose: Drinks can elevate the dining experience. Offering a **variety of both alcoholic and nonalcoholic** options ensures there's something for everyone.

Considerations:

- **Balance:** You should have something for those who prefer alcohol and those who don't. Mocktails can be just as exciting and creative as cocktails.

- **Variety:** In addition to the classics, try to introduce unique beverages, like **fresh fruit sodas** or **spiced teas**, to make the experience more memorable.

- **Pairing:** Ensure your drink choices complement the food. For example, **light, citrusy mocktails** with appetizers, or **spiced cocktails** with rich curries.

Example:

- **Cucumber & Mint Cooler (Mocktail):** A refreshing, cooling drink made with cucumber, mint, and lime perfect for summer.

- **Tamarind Whiskey Sour:** A twist on the classic whiskey sour, made with tamarind syrup for a tangy, savory punch.

5. Specials:

Purpose: Specials keep the menu fresh and evolving. Seasonal offerings or chef's specials add variety and excitement for regular guests.

Considerations:

- **Seasonal Ingredients:** Offer dishes that are inspired by what's fresh and in season, whether it's **winter root vegetables** or **summer fruits**.

- **Creativity:** Specials are your chance to get a little more creative and offer something different from the standard menu.

- **Limited Time Offers:** Exclusivity can make a special dish feel more exciting and in demand.

Example:

- **Winter Truffle Dal Tadka:** A chef's special that takes traditional dal tadka and adds a luxurious truffle infusion for a winter inspired twist.

- **Mango Mousse Tart:** A seasonal special served only during mango season light and refreshing, with the sweet, tropical flavor of ripe mango.

Scenario: Balancing the Menu for a Modern Indian Fusion Restaurant

Imagine a **fusion restaurant** that blends the flavors of India with international techniques and influences, such as **Indian BBQ, continental curries,** and **global desserts.**

For this restaurant, balance could be achieved by offering a range of dishes that incorporate Indian spices in creative ways, while providing options for all kinds of guests whether they prefer lighter, healthier options or more indulgent dishes.

Sample Menu with Balanced Sections:

Appetizers:

- **Chili Cheese Toast with Mango Salsa**

- **Aloo Tikki with Sweet Tamarind Glaze**

- **Vegetable Samosa Bites with Mint Cilantro Chutney**

Mains:

- **Tandoori Lamb Chops with Garlic Butter**

- **Kadhi Pakora with Cilantro Rice**

- **Methi Malai Murg (Fenugreek Cream Chicken)**

Desserts:

- **Kesar Pista Panna Cotta**

- **Chocolate Mousse with Pistachio Crumble**

- **Carrot Halwa with Coconut Ice Cream**

Drinks:

- **Ginger Lemon Fizz (Mocktail)**

- **Spiced Apple Cider (Hot Drink)**

- **Lychee Mojito**

Specials:

- **Mango & Pineapple Salad (Seasonal)**

- **Methi Malai Murg (Chef's Special)**

By balancing these different aspects appetizers, mains, desserts, drinks, and specials you can create a harmonious menu that will appeal to a wide variety of guests and dining preferences.

This menu concept draws inspiration from **Chef Gaggan Anand**, a pioneer in modern Indian fusion cuisine. Chef Anand is known for his innovative, boundary pushing approach at **Gaggan**, his restaurant in Bangkok, which earned multiple accolades, including being listed among the top restaurants in Asia. His menus blend traditional Indian ingredients with modern cooking techniques, creating a dining experience that's both familiar and surprising.

The fusion style, the use of **seasonal ingredients**, and dishes that reflect a deep understanding of Indian flavors, yet experiment with global influences, mirror his culinary philosophy. The menu's balance between rich, comforting main courses, refreshing appetizers, and indulgent desserts echoes his ability to craft experiences that both challenge and delight the diner.

3. Ingredient Accessibility & Cost

When designing a menu, **ingredient accessibility** and **cost** are two crucial factors that can make or break your restaurant's profitability. Understanding these aspects allows you to create a menu that not only tastes great but is also sustainable and cost effective. Below are some guidelines to help you factor in the availability and cost of ingredients in your menu planning:

1. Are the Ingredients Easily Accessible?

If you're working with ingredients that are difficult to source, it can create both logistical challenges and drive up costs. The availability of ingredients can vary depending on where you're located, and using exotic or rare ingredients can be expensive.

Considerations:

- **Local Sourcing:** Whenever possible, try to source ingredients locally. This reduces shipping costs, ensures freshness, and often results in lower food costs. For instance, using local **tomatoes** or **leafy greens** will likely be cheaper than sourcing them from faraway regions.

- **Seasonal Ingredients:** Incorporating **seasonal produce** into your menu can help reduce costs and maintain a fresh variety. For example, using **mangoes** in the summer for salads, smoothies, and desserts is cost effective when they're in season.

Example: Let's say you're working in a **coastal city** where **seafood** is abundant and local. Offering a **seafood platter** that uses locally caught fish, prawns, and crab will reduce transportation costs and keep the menu fresh while supporting local fishermen. On the other hand, if you choose a rare ingredient like **imported lobster**, it might make the dish more expensive and harder to source regularly.

2. Can You Scale the Recipes for Larger Quantities?

When creating dishes, you must consider **how well the recipe scales**. Some recipes may work perfectly for a small batch, but when increased in volume, the cost or quality might change. It's essential to test recipes in small batches before committing to larger quantities for your menu.

Considerations:

- **Batch Testing:** Test recipes in small quantities to ensure the flavor, texture, and cost hold up when scaled. A **curry recipe**, for instance, might require adjusting the seasoning to ensure the flavors remain balanced as you increase the quantity.

- **Portion Control:** Maintain consistency by controlling the portion sizes for each dish. If the portion size varies widely, it can impact both the dining experience and your cost control. For example, a dish like **dal tadka** can be scaled easily by measuring the rice and dal portions accurately.

Example: Let's say you're preparing **Saffron Biryani**. Initially, when testing for small batches, the recipe may call for **500g of rice** and **100g of saffron**. However, when you scale this up to **10kg of rice**, you need to adjust the **saffron proportion** since the delicate flavor of saffron can be overwhelming in large quantities. This scaling can impact the dish's cost, so always test beforehand.

3. What is Your Food Cost for Each Dish?

Understanding the **food cost** for each dish is critical for setting prices and ensuring profitability. A wellpriced dish covers not only the cost of ingredients but also labor, overheads, and other expenses.

Considerations:

- **Ingredient Cost Calculation:** For each dish, calculate the total cost of ingredients used. Don't forget to include small, often overlooked ingredients like spices or garnishes. If you're using **saffron**, for example, it can be expensive so a little goes a long way.

- **Food Cost Percentage:** This is a benchmark for pricing your dishes. A typical food cost percentage in a restaurant should range from **25% to 35%** of the dish price. For example, if a dish costs you ₹100 to make, your selling price should range from ₹285 to ₹400 to maintain a healthy food cost percentage.

Example: Let's say you're creating a dish, **Paneer Tikka.**

- **Ingredients:**
  - Paneer (200g): ₹50
  - Spices & Yogurt: ₹30
  - Garnishes (cilantro, lemon, etc.): ₹10
  - **Total Ingredient Cost:** ₹90

Using the **food cost percentage** formula:
If you want a food cost percentage of 30%, the formula is: **Selling Price = Total Ingredient Cost ÷ Ideal Food Cost Percentage**
Selling Price = ₹90 ÷ 0.30 = ₹300

So, to make a reasonable profit and cover other operational costs, the selling price of **Paneer Tikka** should be ₹300.

Example Scenario: Menu for a Small Cafe

Let's say you're opening a small cafe in an area with a strong **vegetarian** following. You want your menu to reflect both **affordable pricing** and **ingredient accessibility.**

- **Appetizer: Aloo Tikki Chaat**
  Ingredients: Potatoes, chickpea flour, tamarind chutney, spices, yogurt

Cost per serving: ₹40
Selling Price: ₹130
Food Cost Percentage: 30%

- **Main Course: Vegetable Biryani**
  Ingredients: Rice, vegetables, biryani masala, saffron
  Cost per serving: ₹60
  Selling Price: ₹180
  Food Cost Percentage: 33%

- **Dessert: Gulab Jamun**
  Ingredients: Milk powder, ghee, sugar syrup, cardamom
  Cost per serving: ₹20
  Selling Price: ₹70
  Food Cost Percentage: 28%

Final Thoughts:

Ingredient Accessibility and Cost are interdependent and will have a huge impact on your menu's overall success. By focusing on **local sourcing**, **seasonal ingredients**, and proper **scaling**, you can create a menu that balances **cost control** with **creative freedom**. Always **test recipes in small batches** to determine if they can be produced on a larger scale without compromising quality. This approach helps you **stay efficient**, maintain **cost control**, and design a **sustainable menu** for the long term.

4. Keep It Simple, But Memorable

Don't overwhelm your guests with a massive menu.

The Key to a Great Menu:
When designing a menu, simplicity is key. Guests are often overwhelmed by a massive list of options. Instead, focus on a smaller, curated selection of standout dishes that showcase your culinary creativity and keep the dining experience exciting.

The **menu descriptions** should be concise, but also tantalizing, making each dish sound irresistible. Words like **succulent**, **crispy**, **spiced with**, **freshly roasted**, and **seasoned to perfection** can immediately create an image of the dish in the guest's mind.

Let's first look at two examples to better understand how to **keep it simple and memorable**:

Pathetic Menu Example:

Starter:

- **Salad**
  A simple salad with lettuce, cucumber, tomato, and dressing.

Main Course:

- **Chicken Curry**
  Chicken with curry sauce.

Dessert:

- **Ice Cream**
  Vanilla ice cream with some toppings.

Drinks:

- **Water**
  Plain bottled water.

Why It's Pathetic:

- **Boring Descriptions:** There's nothing enticing about the descriptions. These are very generic and fail to excite the guest.

- **Lack of Creativity:** The dishes are overly simplistic and don't showcase any culinary artistry or unique flavors.

- **Missed Opportunity:** The menu doesn't reflect any special or creative elements that would make it memorable for guests.

Ideal Menu Example:

Chef **Nina Chhabra** is known for her modern take on traditional Indian cuisine with a focus on sustainability and vibrant flavors. Here's a sample of her menu:

Starters:

Spiced Roasted Cauliflower Bites
Golden cauliflower tossed in a blend of warm spices, roasted to crispy perfection and served with a tangy tamarind dip.

Chef's Note: *Inspired by the rich flavors of North India, this dish is a perfect balance of smoky, savory, and sweet, ideal for a light bite.*

Main Course:

Mango & Saffron Chicken
Chicken marinated in a sweet, tangy mango and saffron yogurt sauce, grilled until juicy and tender, served with fragrant basmati rice and a drizzle of fresh mint chutney.

Chef's Note: *A fusion of summer flavors with an Indian twist. The saffron adds richness, while the mango brings a refreshing burst of sweetness, making this dish unforgettable.*

Dessert:

Rosewater & Pistachio Kulfi
Fullbodied kulfi made with the finest cream, delicately flavored with rosewater and a touch of pistachio, topped with crushed pistachio crumbs for added crunch.

Chef's Note: *This dessert brings together traditional Indian ice cream with an elegant twist. The delicate floral notes of rose and the rich nuttiness of pistachios create a luscious, meltinyourmouth experience.*

Drinks:

Ginger Lime Fizz
Freshly squeezed lime juice, a hint of ginger syrup, and a fizzy soda finish.

Chef's Note: *A zesty, refreshing drink to cleanse the palate, combining spicy and tangy flavors to pair perfectly with the bold flavors of the dishes.*

Why This Menu Works:

- **Enticing Descriptions:** Each dish is described with vibrant, sensory words that immediately create an image in the guest's mind.

- **Balanced Variety:** The menu offers a variety of textures and flavors, from crunchy and smoky to creamy and tangy, while remaining focused on a smaller number of options.

- **Unique Touch:** The dishes reflect both traditional and contemporary elements, making the menu feel modern and exciting.

- **Chef's Personal Touch:** Chef **Nina Chhabra's** personal notes add character and help connect the dishes to her culinary philosophy, making it more memorable.

The Takeaway:

When designing a menu, remember:

- **Focus on fewer dishes, but make each one stand out.**

- **Be concise with descriptions** and use words that evoke **taste and texture.**

- Keep the **theme and creativity** at the fore front ensure your dishes feel like a curated, cohesive experience rather than a random selection.

- **Add a personal touch** from the chef to make the dishes feel authentic and memorable.

This approach ensures that the menu isn't overwhelming but rather enticing, making it easier for guests to choose and enjoy their meal while also offering something special and unique.

5. Visual Flow & Layout

Design your menu like you design a plate **balanced, aesthetically pleasing, and easy to follow**. A chaotic menu layout can confuse customers and make them unsure of what to order.

As a budding chef, designing a menu isn't just about putting together dishes; it's about presenting your ideas clearly, with an organized structure that resonates with your culinary vision. Whether you're creating a sample menu for a trial or planning a real-life food business, the layout and visual flow play a huge role in making your menu look professional and appealing.

1. Group Items Logically:

The first step in menu design is grouping your dishes logically. This makes it easier for you (and others) to follow the flow of the meal and helps guests, or judges, quickly understand your options. As a chef, think about how you want your dishes to be perceived:

- **Appetizers:** These should be light, exciting, and stimulate the palate. Think fresh, small portions that get the taste buds ready for the main event.

- **Mains:** This is where the heart of your menu lies these dishes should be rich, satisfying, and reflective of your skills. It's your opportunity to showcase your creativity.

- **Desserts:** These can be light, refreshing, or indulgent, depending on the type of meal you're curating. A good dessert adds the finishing touch to your experience.

- **Drinks:** Always consider offering both alcoholic and nonalcoholic options, or even a unique, signature drink to complement your theme. Mocktails, juices, or infused waters can work well.

Example Menu Layout:

Appetizers:

- **Spicy Mango & Avocado Salad**
Tossed with chili lime dressing, fresh cilantro, and roasted sesame seeds.
₹150

- **Crispy Tofu Bites with Tamarind Dip**
Marinated tofu fried to perfection, paired with a tangy tamarind chutney.
₹180

Mains:

- **Spiced Paneer Tikka**
Marinated paneer cubes grilled in a rich blend of Indian spices, served with mint chutney.
₹300

- **Lemon Herb Chicken Breast**
Grilled chicken marinated in a lemony, garlicky sauce, served with sautéed vegetables and mashed potatoes.
₹350

Drinks:

- **Mango Lemonade**
Fresh mango puree with lemon, mint, and a touch of sweetness.
₹120

- **Masala Chai Latte**
Classic Indian spiced tea with steamed milk.
₹100

Why It Works:
Each section is clearly marked and easy to navigate, offering a variety of options in terms of appetizers, mains, and drinks. For budding chefs, presenting a balanced and logical flow will show your organization and ability to craft a complete dining experience.

2. Use White Space for Clarity:

When designing your menu, it's essential to give each dish room to breathe. Just like in plating, **white space** on your menu allows the content to shine without overwhelming your audience. White space also enhances readability and gives the menu a more professional feel.

Example:

Imagine if all your menu items were packed together with no spacing between them. It would be hard to follow and look cluttered. Instead, leaving a little room between categories and items makes everything feel more organized and easier to digest.

Before:
Appetizers Spicy Mango & Avocado Salad Tamarind Dip...

After:
Appetizers:

- **Spicy Mango & Avocado Salad**
  Tossed with chili lime dressing, fresh cilantro, and roasted sesame seeds.
  ₹150

- **Crispy Tofu Bites with Tamarind Dip**
  Marinated tofu fried to perfection, paired with a tangy tamarind chutney.
  ₹180

Why It Works:
The use of spacing between items and sections ensures that the menu looks polished and professional. This layout makes it easier for anyone to skim and understand the content quickly.

3. Choose Readable Fonts:

The fonts you choose should not only match the vibe of your food but also be easy to read. You don't want your creativity in the kitchen to be overshadowed by difficulttoread fonts. For budding chefs, simplicity is key when it comes to menu typography.

Tips:

- Use **clear, professional fonts** such as a simple serif or sans serif font for the main body of your menu.

- Use a **different font** or styling for section headings (Appetizers, Mains, Drinks) to separate categories.

- Avoid too many fonts **one to two fonts** is ideal to maintain consistency and professionalism.

  Example:

- **Main Dish Fonts:** Use a **classic sans** like Arial or Helvetica for clarity.

- **Heading Fonts:** You can experiment with a slightly more decorative font, like a serif font, but keep it legible.

  Why It Works:
  Consistent fonts that are easy to read will allow the dishes to shine without distractions. The clearer and simpler the fonts, the more professional your menu will appear.

4. Reflect Your Personal Style and Culinary Vision:

As a budding chef, your menu layout should also reflect your personal style. Whether you're going for a **modern fusion vibe** or a **traditional comfort food** feel, your menu should express who you are as a chef. Choose fonts, colors, and design elements that align with your overall theme.

Example: If you're designing a modern fusion menu, you might use **sleek, minimalistic design** elements with bold fonts and clean lines. If your focus is on comfort food, the design could be more rustic, with warm colors and a hand written style font that feels personal.

Your Personal Vibe Example:

- **Modern Fusion Menu Layout:**
  A clean white background with **bold typography** for dish names and **understated icons** next to dish descriptions. Subtle splashes of color might be used to highlight the seasonality of the ingredients.

- **Comfort Food Menu Layout:**
  A warm, earthy background with a **hand written style font** for a more inviting, homey feel. Illustrations of food or rustic elements (like wood textures or herbs) could tie the menu together.

Design your menu to reflect your **personal style** and the **culinary experience** you want to offer, while keeping things clean and organized.

Remember, as a budding chef, your menu isn't just a list of dishes it's a reflection of your culinary identity and vision. So take the time to design it thoughtfully and creatively.

6. Think Pairings

Consider wine, mocktails, or even teas that pair well with each dish. If you're offering mains like a spicy tandoori chicken, pair it with a refreshing mint chutney or a **light, crisp cocktail** with a citrus kick. Or, if you're offering rich desserts like a saffron cake, a lightly spiced chai can complement the flavors.

7. Menu Pricing

Pricing isn't just about multiplying costs. It's about understanding your audience, the type of establishment, and **what's fair** for both the customer and the business.

- **What is your ideal food cost percentage?**

- **What is the average**

- **price point for your target market?**

For instance, a fine dining restaurant might price a single entrée at ₹800–₹1500, whereas a casual eatery would price it between ₹300–₹600. Find your market, and price accordingly.

Pro Tip: Ask for Feedback

Don't be afraid to **test your menu** with friends, family, or even strangers. See what resonates and what doesn't. Feedback is crucial to perfecting the taste and structure of your menu before it goes live.

Chapter 9: Plating & Presentation for Trials

A plate should excite the eye before it satisfies the palate.

Why Presentation Matters (Even in Trials)

Even if it's a test run in your home kitchen or a college, how you present your food tells people:
"I *care* about this."

It's not about fancy ingredients or expensive tool sit's about intention, balance, and art.

Plating Basics for Beginners

1. Choose the Right Plate

- **White plates** are classic they let the food pop.

- **Dark or matte finishes** create drama.

- Size matters: don't let the food get lost or feel crammed.

Example: A lemon thyme risotto served in a shallow black stone bowl makes the yellow shine and adds rustic warmth.

2. Placement and Portion

- The clock method: Place your protein at 6 o'clock, veg at 10, starch at 2.

- Think of height stacking adds dimension.

- Odd numbers of components (3 prawns, 5 potato wedges) are more visually appealing than even ones.

3. Color Contrast

Vary textures and colors to make a dish vibrant.

- Use pickled onions for pink

- Edible flowers for freshness

- Mint oil or beetroot purée to paint the plate

Example: Chef Garima Arora's beetroot and berry chaat at Gaa looks like edible art. Simple elements, powerful color.

4. Garnish with Purpose

Don't just sprinkle coriander on everything!
Use:

- **Microgreens** or finely chopped herbs

- **Toasted seeds** for crunch

- **Flavored oils, zests,** or **spice dusts** to enhance aroma

Tip: Keep garnishes edible and intentional. No plastic flowers or random lettuce!

5. Keep It Real

During trials, focus on how long your plating holds:

- Does the sauce bleed into other elements?

- Do crispy things go soggy in 5 minutes?

- Can this survive 5 plates in a row?

Real Life Chef Tip:

Chef Hussain Shahzad (The Bombay Canteen, O Pedro) says:

"I plate like I'm telling a story. You've got to be clear with your language don't mumble on the plate."

Trial Tip:

Take photos of every trial plate from different angles. Compare what works. Ask:

- Does it look appetizing from above?

- Does it tell a story?

- Would *I* be excited to eat this?

Chapter 10: Naming Your Dishes

"Words are the garnish before the first bite."

Why Naming Matters

The name of your dish is often the first thing your guest hears or reads it builds curiosity, emotion, and expectation. A good name can:

- Make a dish sound irresistible

- Tell a story or highlight an ingredient

- Reflect your personality or culinary style

3 Naming Styles That Work

1. Ingredient Driven

Focus on the hero ingredients to keep it clear and elegant.

Examples:

- **Smoked Brinjal with Yogurt Foam**

- **Millet Risotto with Lemongrass**

Tip: This is great for tasting menus or minimalist fine dining.

2. Memory or Place Based

Tie it to a memory, place, or personal story this makes it poetic and emotional.

Examples:

- **Sunday at Ajji's** (for a comforting jackfruit curry)

- **By the Backwaters** (inspired by a Keralastyle seafood broth)

- **Train Station Cutlet** (a nostalgic potato cutlet like ones sold at Indian railway platforms)

Tip: Great for popups and storytellingdriven menus.

3. Whimsical or Fun

Add humor or wordplaybut stay rooted in the food's reality.

Examples:

- **Lassi but Make it Sexy** (a lassiinspired dessert)

- **Ant Bite** – A reinterpretation of Pavlova with ants, from **Chef Johnson Ebenezer** at Farmlore

- **The OG Pongal 2.0** – A modern plated take on classic pongal

Tip: This works beautifully for modern, casual, or fusion concepts.

When Naming, Ask Yourself:

- Does this reflect the soul of the dish?

- Is it intriguing but not confusing?

- Can someone visualize the flavor, texture, or story from just the name?

Chef Insight:

Chef Thomas Zacharias (The Locavore, formerly Bombay Canteen):

"A dish name is like the first sentence of a short story. It should pull the diner in."

Try This Exercise:

Name the following dish using each of the three styles:

A dish of masala rubbed grilled pineapple, coconut foam, and toasted mustard seeds.

Chapter 11: The Art of Fusion without Confusion

"Fusion isn't confusion when done with intention."

What is Fusion?

Fusion cooking is about blending elements from different cuisines to create something new, bold, and personal. But it's easy to go wrong when you don't understand the roots or flavors you're mixing.

Fusion ≠ Random

Wrong Way:
Throwing sushi rice, peri peri sauce, and paneer into a taco and calling it "global."
Right Way:
Respecting techniques, understanding flavor profiles, and finding balance between cultures.

3 Golden Rules of Thoughtful Fusion

1. Know the Originals

Understand the **basics** of both cuisines flavor structure, cooking techniques, and purpose.

Example: Before creating a *Miso Butter Naan*, know how **naans** are tandoor cooked and how **miso butter** behaves under heat.

2. Find a Connector

A common ingredient, method, or emotional thread helps tie the two cuisines.

Example:

- **Kokum + Lemongrass** → tropical & acidic

- **Tamarind + Soy Sauce** → umami and sour

- **Butter Chicken Pizza** → combines indulgence + familiarity

- **Biryani Arancini** by **Chef Prateek Sadhu** Italian technique, Indian soul

3. Stay Grounded

Ask: Would someone from each culture feel honored, not mocked, by this dish?

Chef Johnson Ebenezer at Farm lore does it brilliantly with his "Ant Pavlova" and "Smoked Plantain Tart"modernist, yet rooted in terroir.

Fusion Success Stories

- **Chef Manu Chandra's** Bhuna Ghee Roast Bao

- **Gaggan Anand's** Lick It Up Indian street flavor, modern art

- **The Bombay Canteen's** Keema Pao Tacos

- Your own college experiments with **Rasam Ramen** or **Kheer Cheesecake**

Fusion Flops to Avoid

- Mismatched textures: creamy + dry

- Overpowering ingredients: wasabi + garlic + chili calm down.

- Too many ideas on one plate. Simplicity is still king.

Thought Starter:

"What dish represents you? Could you fuse that with your favorite international dish while keeping both souls alive?"

Chapter 12: The Sustainable Chef's Mindset

In a world that celebrates speed, perfection, and production, being a chef today demands more than just skill it requires mindfulness. Sustainability is no longer just about where you source your ingredients from; it's about how you sustain **yourself** and your **kitchen** for the long run.

Mindful Sourcing: Local, Seasonal, Minimal Waste

Sustainability starts at the roots literally. Choosing **local** and **seasonal** produce doesn't just reduce your carbon footprint; it also supports your community and keeps your dishes in tune with nature's rhythm.

- **Local doesn't mean boring.** It means fresher produce, deeper flavor, and a real story behind every carrot or chili.

- **Seasonal menus force creativity.** You won't always have strawberries or avocados. You'll find new ways to use jackfruit, gooseberries, pumpkin, or radish topsturning kitchen scraps into conversation starters.

- **Minimal waste is a mindset.** Learn to use *everything*: broccoli stems, coriander roots, leftover ghee solids, rice water. Make it a challenge, not a chore.

Example: Chef Thomas Zacharias (formerly of The Bombay Canteen) made ugly vegetables cool again. His "The Locavore" project encourages chefs to buy hyperlocal, forgotten ingredients and turn them into star dishes.

Managing Stress & Staying Grounded

Chefs often wear stress like a badge of honor. But exhaustion, aggression, and chaos don't have to be the default. A sustainable mindset means respecting the **human** behind the apron.

- Build rituals that calm you music while prepping, 10 deep breaths before service, journaling after a tough day.

- Rest is productive. A burnt out chef won't create their best work.

- Keep your station organized. A cluttered space leads to a cluttered mind.

- Know when to ask for help. Delegating isn't weak nessit's leadership.

Example: Chef Garima Arora (Gaa, Bangkok) advocates for grace under pressure and emotional resilience. Her leadership style blends sharp discipline with empathy and open dialogue.

Balancing Ambition with Self Care

You want to make it big. That's great. But not at the cost of burning out before you arrive.

- Say no to toxic hustle culture. 20hour shifts every day are not a flex.

- Eat your own food. Hydrate. Rest. Move your body.

- Success that costs your health or peace isn't success it's survival.

The **real flex** is showing up in the kitchen consistently, creatively, and joyfully.

Chef Wisdom: Real Practices That Work

Here are some smart habits shared by chefs who've learned to sustain both the planet and themselves:

- **Chef Johnson Ebenezer** (Farmlore, Bengaluru): Builds menus around what the farm gives that week. No set menu. Just trust and talent.

- **Chef Ritu Dalmia**: Uses conscious sourcing and minimalist menus to reduce waste while highlighting honest flavors.

- **Chef Anahita Dhondy**: Advocates for ancient grains like millets, reducing reliance on water heavy crops like rice and wheat.

Being a sustainable chef is not about being perfect. It's about making small, powerful choices that nourish you, your guests, and your planet. Remember: your creativity is renewable, but only if you are too.

Cook with care. Create with clarity. Sustain with soul.

Chapter 13: Hosting Your First Tasting Table or Pop Up

So, your recipes are tested, your plating is sharp, and your concept is clear. Now it's time to step out of the safe zone and into the real world by hosting a **tasting table** or **popup**. This chapter is your guide to bringing your food to a live audience.

I've attended two food trials so far each one teaching me something unique.

The first was at **The Leela Bhartiya City**, where I was given a structured Indian menu: plain rice, one chicken starter, a fish-based main course, and a dal. I carefully designed the menu to show my familiarity with regional Indian flavors. I served **tandoori chicken tikka**, **meen moilee** (a coastal fish curry), **steamed white rice**, and **palak dal**. I chose palak dal to bring contrast in both flavor and color, avoiding repetition on the plate.

The result? Pure joy. The **Executive Chef Rajesh Roy** nearly finished half the food on his own it was one of the most affirming moments of my journey. What helped me succeed was a **trial day** I did earlier with the same menu, collecting feedback and adjusting accordingly. Today, I hold a **Hotel Operational Trainee offer** from The Leela. Planning and preparation truly pay off.

The second trial was at **The Oberoi**, and it came with a twist: *freedom to design my own menu*. I wanted to highlight an underrepresented cuisine, so I chose **Tibetan food**. My menu included:

- **Soup:** Thukpa

- **Starter:** Shabalay (deep-fried meat pastry)

- **Main Course:** Beef Shapta

- **Bread:** Tingmo

- **Dessert:** Bhatsa Markhu

I had reinvented Thukpa based on a Chinese-style version I had at a small eatery clear bone broth with tofu, coriander, noodles, and chilli oil. My dessert, Bhatsa Markhu, was a chewy flour dumpling with a brown sugar, butter, and ginger emulsion.

This time, I didn't have a **trial day or feedback round** before the final tasting and that overconfidence may have played a part in the result. Sometimes, *believing too much in the idea without grounding it in execution* can backfire.

The **Executive Sous Chef Gaurav** gave thoughtful feedback. He said that while the concept was unique, the **execution and storytelling didn't align**.

"It's not famous for a reason because it's not always palatable. The thought is right, but the food isn't."

He was right. If I say I'm presenting authentic Tibetan cuisine, I need to honor its flavor profile. While I was trying to elevate or reinterpret, I ended up **muting the essence**.

I didn't get the best score, but I walked away with clarity. That day reminded me:
Preparation isn't just physical it's mental and culinary alignment too.

And honestly? Sometimes you win, sometimes you learn. You never lose.

Why Do a Tasting or Pop-Up?

- **Low risk, high feedback:** You learn what works and what doesn't without investing lakhs.

- **Realtime reactions:** People will tell you what they felt before you even ask.

- **Build your name:** Create buzz, grow your following, and get noticed.

- **Connect with your diners:** You'll build loyalty and community, one plate at a time.

Planning It Right

1. Set a Clear Goal:

- Are you testing new dishes?

- Want to experiment with a theme or cuisine?

- Trying to gauge demand for a future café or cloud kitchen?

2. Choose the Right Format:

- **Tasting Table:** Invite 8–12 people for a seated meal with feedback.

- **Pop Up:** A limited time setup in a café, park, or terrace open to the public or prebooked guests.

3. Pick a Venue:

- Collaborate with cafés or coworking kitchens.

- Use your college space or someone's home with a good setup.

- Consider delivery based popups for broader reach.

What to Serve?

- **Stick to 3–6 dishes.** Show range, but don't overburden yourself.

- **Include a drink (mocktail or cooler)** to elevate the meal.

- **Balance the flow:** Start light, build flavor, end with comfort.

Tip: Design dishes that can be quickly plated and served warm. Avoid things that wilt or split easily.

feedback That Fuels Growth

- Give your guests a simple form (paper or Google Form).

Ask:

- What stood out?

- What felt off or confusing?

- Would you order this again?

- One word to describe this dish?

Golden rule: Accept criticism with curiosity, not defensiveness.

Make It Memorable

- Take photos and videos while you cook, serve, and engage.

- Record honest reactions these become your testimonials and content.

- Share your story behind the event why it mattered.

Chef Vanshika Bhatia started with private tasting dinners in Gurgaon before launching OMO. Those small gatherings helped refine her earthy, modern Indian food style.

Chef Saransh Goila grew his Goila Butter Chicken brand from a series of kitchen trials, feedback meals, and strategic popups before franchising.

You don't need a restaurant to be a chef. All you need is a table, a few hungry hearts, and the courage to serve what you believe in.

Chapter 14: From Notes to Network

You've been sketching recipes, testing dishes, tweaking sauces, scribbling in journals, and saving plating inspo now it's time to transform those *notes* into a *network*. This chapter shows how to document your journey, build your brand, and connect with fellow chefs and food lovers.

Step 1: Keep a Chef's Notebook (Digitally or Physically)

- Track **ingredients, ratios, temperatures, failures**, and **feedback**.

- Note your **inspirations** a quote, a memory, a street food moment, a smell.

- Sketch out plating ideas or take progress pics after every trial.

- Build your personal **"Flavor Bible"**: which flavors pair well, which don't.

A messy book is a sign of a creative chef.

Step 2: Document on Social Media

Whether it's Instagram, LinkedIn, YouTube Shorts, or a blog your content becomes your resume.

- Show behind the scenes: trials, fails, and breakthroughs.

- Post dish stories: Why you made it. Who inspired it.

- Share *before and after*: raw ideas to refined plating.

 Tip: Don't just post food. Post thought. People connect to purpose, not just pretty plates.

Step 3: Engage with the Culinary Community

- Follow other young chefs, home cooks, and industry leaders.

- Comment, share, support their work it comes back.

- Attend food fests, chef panels, and popups.

- Join chef WhatsApp/Telegram groups or Discord servers ideas multiply when shared.

Real Chef, Real Growth

Chef Hussain Shahzad (O Pedro, Bombay Canteen) started by posting small, detailed photos of dishes he was testing, with honest captions. Over time, his raw storytelling caught the attention of big names in the industry.

Chef Amninder Sandhu grew her community by sharing her experiments with traditional open fire cooking, long before it became trendy. She didn't chase followers; she built connection.

Tools to Use:

- **Google Sheets or Notion:** Recipe costing + kitchen prep logs.

- **Canva or Adobe Express:** For social posts or menus.

- **VSCO or Lightroom Mobile:** Light photo editing.

- **Instagram/Facebook Creator Tools:** Schedule and analyze content.

"Your network is your net worth, but only if your work is worth the connection."

The more authentically you share, the stronger your network grows.

Chapter 15: The Courage to Create (Again)

As a chef, your creativity will be tested your flavors, your style, your vision. At times, it will feel like the universe is not on your side. You'll mess up. Your food might not turn out right. Your plating might look like a hot mess. And that's okay. This chapter is all about having the courage to face those setbacks and keep going, again and again.

The Reality of Creative Blocks

It happens to every chef. You'll hit a wall.

- The flavor doesn't click.

- Your inspiration runs dry.

- You wonder if you should quit.

But here's the thing: *that's part of the process*.

It's those struggles that push you to rethink, rework, and reimagine your craft. Every failed dish is a lesson. Every misstep is an opportunity for growth.

"There's no such thing as failure, only feedback." – Chef Gusteau, *Ratatouille*.

How to Bounce Back

1. **Step away** from the kitchen when it gets too much. Sometimes the best way to solve a problem is to give your mind a break.

2. **Reflect** on what worked in the past. What were the dishes you were most proud of? What inspired them? Can you bring that magic back?

3. **Experiment without the pressure** of getting it perfect. Sometimes, just throwing a few flavors together and seeing where it goes can be the key to rediscovery.

4. **Seek feedback** whether from a mentor, a fellow chef, or even your tasting table. Sometimes, all it takes is a fresh perspective to spark a breakthrough.

Keep Creating, Keep Evolving

The world of food is constantly changing. New trends, new flavors, new techniques. If you want to stay relevant, you need to stay curious and keep creating.

Chef Narisara Vichit, who specializes in Thai cuisine, once said: *"Creativity in food isn't just about coming up with new dishes; it's about giving something old a new twist."*

And that's the heart of a chef's journey: the constant evolution.

Take the Leap

Don't be afraid to experiment with new ingredients, styles, or techniques. Even if you fail, those trials will get you closer to your culinary identity.

"Success is the sum of small efforts, repeated day in and day out." – Robert Collier

Embrace the courage to create and recreate because *the world needs your flavor*.

The End is Just the Beginning

You've got the foundation, the mindset, and the tools to succeed. Now it's your time to experiment, to create your signature dishes, and to take your culinary journey to new heights.

The true measure of a chef is not how many dishes they can make, but how many times they can rise from failure, stronger than before.

A Final Note from the Author

As I wrap up this journey, I want to thank you for taking the time to dive into these pages. Every lesson, every recipe, and every piece of advice has been drawn from the real, raw moments of my culinary pat from the thrill of trials at The Leela and The Oberoi, to the sting of failure in my first competition, to the triumph of returning stronger the next year. These stories aren't just memories; they are milestones that shaped my growth.

This book would not be complete without a note of gratitude to the technology that helped bring it to life. I embraced AI not as a shortcut, but as a creative companion helping me reflect, refine, and structure my thoughts into something I could proudly share. Just like a sharp knife or a well-seasoned pan, AI became a tool in my kitchen not to replace the cook, but to empower the storyteller.

The road to becoming a chef is not easy. There will be highs and lows, moments of doubt, and moments of triumph. But through it all, remember that the true beauty of cooking lies not just in the perfect dish, but in the passion, the love, and the purpose you bring to the kitchen.

You are not just creating food you are telling a story, sharing a part of yourself, and leaving a mark on the world. I encourage you to experiment, to fail, and to keep pushing forward, because the greatest chefs are not those who never fail, but those who never give up.

Here's to the boldness in your cooking, the courage in your creativity, and the joy in your culinary journey. Keep cooking with purpose, and I look forward to seeing the flavors you'll bring to life.

Until then, may your kitchen be filled with inspiration and your heart with the courage to create.

With love and love,
Maneesh Kumar :)